T0062011

365
MICRO-
MOMENTS
to BRING
you JOY

For Emma: a day, a year,
a life of good things.

Jason Ward

365
MICRO-
MOMENTS
to BRING
you JOY

OH EDITIONS

"One hears it without listening as one breathes without thinking. But to a listening ear the sound disintegrates into many different notes–the slow slap of a loch, the high clear trill of a rivulet, the roar of spate. On one short stretch of burn the ear may distinguish a dozen different notes at once."

Nan Shepherd, *The Living Mountain*

"How great is it to find a few stray bonus fries at the bottom of your McDonald's bag?"

Amy Krouse Rosenthal, *Encyclopedia of an Ordinary Life*

One of the rules of history, the writer Michael Bywater noted, is that people don't write about what is too obvious to mention. The information, having never been recorded, is accordingly lost for ever. The same principle applies to joy. We're encouraged to judge personal fulfilment in terms of goals and milestones, but our actual lives are constructed out of much smaller pieces: cardigans, daffodils, pub gardens on summer afternoons. Reading by a window as it snows outside. Fresh spaghetti tossed in olive oil. Kissing in photobooths. Murmurations of birds. The warmth of the sun on the tops of your shoulders.

It's these undiscussed pleasures, so modest it's possible to never think directly about their existence, that give life texture and meaning. Their slightness makes them easy to overlook, but that's the very thing that also makes them special. Life is difficult and tragic, but it's also filled with all of these good things, all of the time. Paying attention to such joys can improve your own life by allowing space – making space – for what's small and silly and special about being alive. It does the soul good.

SPRING

Walking down a street and being showered by falling cherry blossoms.

When sunlight catches the bottom
of a swimming pool.

SPRING

Smushing tomatoes in the pan
with the back of a wooden spoon.

The bit during a car wash when the brushes close in and it feels like you're under the sea.

Being woken up by the sound of birds singing.

A sense that the days are finally starting to get longer.

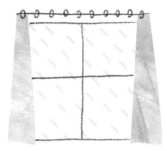

Reading a book when the only sound is rain pattering against the windows.

Wild garlic.

SPRING

A cat that lives nearby and that in a weird way you sort of consider a neighbour.

Buying yourself an Easter egg and eating the whole thing, even though Easter is weeks away.

When a friend cancels plans but it's okay because it means you get an evening to yourself.

Spotting a much-needed pub
in the distance after a long, long
walk in the country.

The first few bites of a pancake.

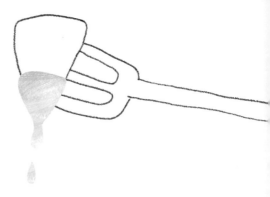

A sudden rush of colourful fields on a train journey.

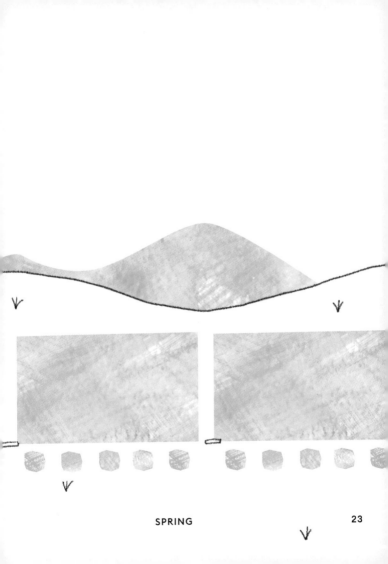

SPRING

Suddenly remembering
you've made yourself a cup
of tea and finding it's at the
perfect temperature.

Finding a photograph you've
never seen before of a parent when
they were young.

An irrational but deeply felt attachment to your favourite mug.

Getting into a bed that has freshly laundered sheets.

When it's warm enough that you've stopped putting the heating on.

Sitting on a ferry, watching the mainland get smaller.

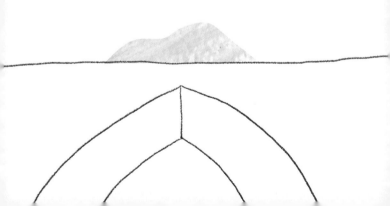

People and what they can do,
instead of money and what
it can buy.

Old stone walls.

The shimmering reflection of
water on the underside of a bridge.

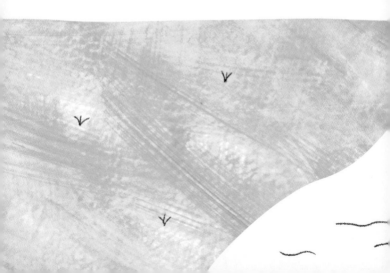

Visiting a museum and the ten minutes you spend daydreaming about quitting your job to become an Egyptologist.

A dog in the office for a day.

Butter melting over
a hot cross bun.

SPRING

The sparkling brightness
of a freshly mopped kitchen.

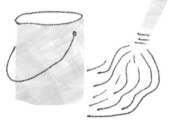

Using an old-fashioned lift where you have to close the door yourself.

When someone brings you flowers for no specific reason other than they wanted to do something nice.

Being in a sauna and feeling like
you could be in Finland.

The smell of just-blown-out
birthday candles.

Getting your washing in just before it starts pouring down.

SPRING

When you put your big coat
in the closet, hopefully to
remain until the autumn.

Watching a bird on a branch
out of your window.

SPRING

A glass of wine in the bath.

The Eurovision Song Contest!

Getting a starter *and* a dessert, like you're someone who should be wearing ermine and initiating the Reformation.

The warm crackle before
a record starts playing.

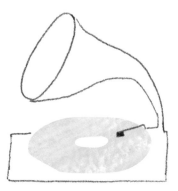

SPRING

Motes of dust floating
in a sunbeam.

A home filled with plants.

SPRING

Spotting a fox on your street,
late at night.

SPRING

A hug when you need a hug.

When you visit a friend and notice that they've put up a postcard you once sent them.

SPRING

Sitting at a table outside a cafe,
watching the world go by.

A baby asleep in the crook
of your arm.

The fastest line at the
supermarket.

Walking alone in nature and suddenly realising that you can't hear a single sound, and that the silence is enormously comforting.

Impulsively deciding
to have a picnic.

When you think the shampoo bottle is empty but it ends up lasting for another week.

Lying on the sofa in the afternoon, drifting off into a light but restful sleep.

A well-stocked spice rack.

The giddy relief as you make your train with just moments to spare.

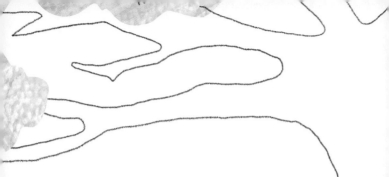

Sitting in the shade of an exceptionally grand tree.

A pillow that is precisely to your tastes, fluffiness-wise.

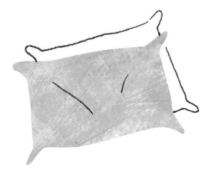

Visiting the library to pick
up one book and leaving with
an armful of them.

The way that cola from a glass
bottle just tastes better.

SPRING

Being struck, profoundly
and all at once, by the beauty
of the season.

After a cold, rainy walk, jumping straight in a piping hot shower.

A big night out for the first
time in forever.

When your friend is wearing
something you bought them
as a gift years ago.

Making a sandwich which
is very nearly perfect.

A long bike ride with no particular destination in mind.

Stretching out on a bed,
as big as you can.

When you get in from
a tiring day and someone
offers to cook for you.

Eating biscuits fresh out of the oven before they've even cooled.

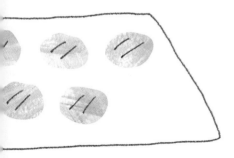

SPRING

A little sun when you're
in need of it.

Catching the scent of flowers
on the breeze.

SPRING

When you drop your phone and
the screen doesn't break.

Receiving a piece of genuinely good advice that feels like a gift.

Getting home from work exhausted and knowing you have nothing else you need to do for the rest of the day.

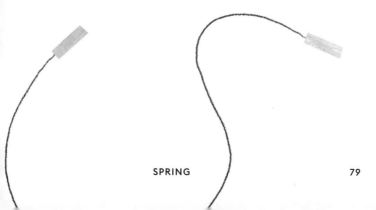

After getting some exercise,
the feeling that you can
do absolutely anything.

Completely rearranging your food cupboards and suddenly finding you have much more room.

When you're on a long journey and there's only one more stop before you arrive.

Going to bed and not needing
to set an alarm for the morning.

The instinctive kindness of people
towards strangers in need.

Bread that's so good you
don't even need butter.

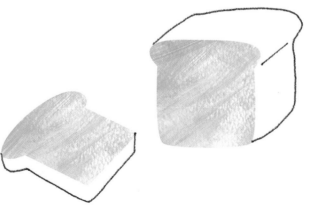

SPRING

Rereading one of your
favourite books and finding
a meaningful sentence
you've underlined in pencil.

When you pour water from the washing up bowl into the sink and the bowl floats around for a minute like a boat.

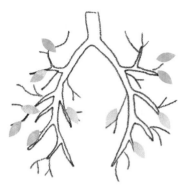

Taking a deep lungful of clean air
that makes it briefly feel like all
your atoms have rearranged.

When you bake a cake and
it doesn't sink in the oven.

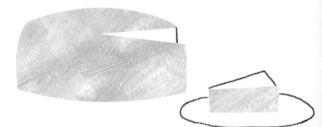

Having no plans for the day more elaborate than watching a couple of movies, sprawled out on the sofa.

When you have just enough time for another cup of tea before you need to leave the house.

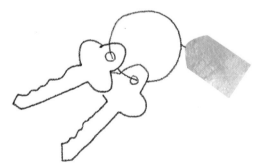

SPRING

The way that buses sound better
in the rain.

Making a huge spontaneous
decision and immediately knowing
it's the right course.

When you have a day off work
and you do as little as possible.

An anniversary that
no one else knows about.

When your favourite song hasn't
been played at a gig, but then the
band come back on and do it as
an encore.

When you're really thirsty and you drink straight from the tap like you're the tiger who came to tea.

SPRING

Camping with a friend and barely getting any sleep because you spend half the night talking and making each other laugh.

Sitting on a pebbly beach,
eating a bag of chips.

A sky ablush with stars.

SPRING

Leaving work while it's still light outside.

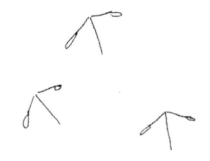

The way that springtime never
fails to make you feel hopeful.

SUMMER

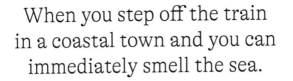

When you step off the train
in a coastal town and you can
immediately smell the sea.

Briefly falling asleep with your head on someone's shoulder.

Green ink.

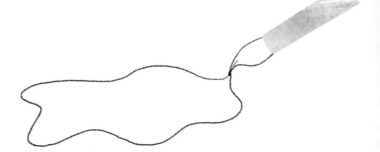

When it's warm
enough that
you don't need
to take a jacket.

Freewheeling down
a hill that you've cycled
to the top of.

Unexpected cake.

SUMMER

The way that sunblock smells
precisely like summer.

Secretly drinking wine
in the cinema.

Diving into a deep, dark lake
and feeling your skin adjust
to the cold water.

Bare feet on warm sand.

SUMMER

The soft rustle of wind
through trees.

When they wash your hair at the hairdressers and it feels unspeakably luxurious.

A late-night bowl of cereal.

Swimming in a river,
floating in the sea.

When you stick your hand
out of the car window and make
waves with your fingers.

An evening walk down a country lane dappled with the shadows of tree leaves.

Receiving an actual handwritten
letter in the post.

Kissing under streetlamps.

SUMMER

Independent bookshops.

A summer morning when the world feels alive with possibility.

SUMMER

Going on holiday primarily
so you can read on a beach.

A work of art in a gallery that you return to again and again, like a pilgrimage.

Standing at the edge of the ocean,
trying to imagine its size.

☼   ☼   ☼

Going straight to the park
after work.

When you have exactly enough
change for something.

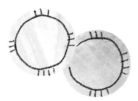

Tea in a proper teacup with
a saucer, and a biscuit or two
(probably two).

The cool side of the pillow.

When a cat that was previously suspicious of you comes over and sits on your lap.

Discovering a remarkable
new writer and it's like
learning a secret.

The peal
of church bells.
Also the word "peal".

When the setting sun
catches a building and it's awash
with tangerine.

Unlikely animal friendships.

Waking up in a sun-flooded bed,
the whole weekend in front of you.

An ice-cold shower
on a really hot day.

☀ ☀ ☀

Going to see one of your
favourite musicians and knowing
the words to every song.

Walking along the edge of the shore with your shoes off.

A chocolate bar in your bag
that you'd forgotten was there,
and it's not even squashed.

Finding a photobooth
that still lets you take four
different pictures.

The smell of pine trees
on a warm day.

SUMMER

When you have an empty seat next to you for the whole journey.

A tiny, quizzical bird following
you around your garden.

Sitting on the bank of a river with a drink in your hand.

When the whole room
is lit up by lightning.

The smell of a barbecue as you walk down the street.

SUMMER

A field blooming with wild flowers.

When you've made a great
packed lunch and all morning
you're excited about eating it.

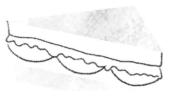

Getting out of the water and
letting the sun dry you.

Watching a dog with very floppy ears dig a hole on the beach.

☀ ☀ ☀

The moment when you're sitting in the cinema and the lights dim.

Finishing an ice cream
before it melts
down your hand.

The valiant optimism with
which you first approach
an all-you-can-eat buffet.

SUMMER

Lying in a patch of afternoon
sunlight like a lazy cat.

Seeing an old friend and suddenly all feels right with the world.

When you set your out-of-office reply and in that instant you feel like you're (finally!) on holiday.

Waking up and you don't have
a single plan or obligation:
the day is completely open
and waiting for you.

When someone brings you
a cup of tea and you didn't
even ask for one.

Wriggling out of a tent in your sleeping bag to watch the stars.

Looking out of an aeroplane
window as the land gives way
to the ocean.

A bag of sugary doughnuts
bought at the end of a pier.

When you read a sentence
so immaculate it stays in your
head forever.

Sitting by a bonfire at
a party, deep in conversation
and wholly alive.

That moment at the height
of summer when you get excited
by the idea of regularly wearing
jumpers again.

Completing a crossword.

☀ ☀ ☀

When you get around to a task
you've been putting off, and it
turns out you don't actually need
to do anything.

A cool breeze when it's
unreasonably hot.

Being woken
up by a thundestorm.

SUMMER

When a friend mentions a tiny
detail from your life that
you wouldn't think anyone might
remember except you.

The feeling of grass beneath
your feet.

Listening to the ocean at night,
the waves crashing softly against
the shore.

Unexpectedly receiving a thank you card in the post.

☼   ☼   ☼

The late-night camaraderie of slightly drunk strangers at a festival.

Packing a suitcase for
your holiday, and it mostly
contains books.

Being deep within a forest and feeling genuine mystery.

Drinking a cocktail and briefly feeling much fancier than you know you really are.

The complex and entirely internal ranking system you have for your crockery.

Lying in the grass and watching the clouds, feeling perfectly content.

When sunlight dances on water
and it looks like wild electricity.

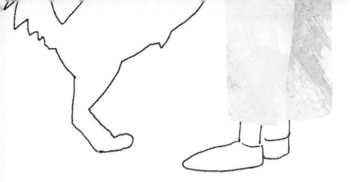

A dog that greets you like
it already knows you.

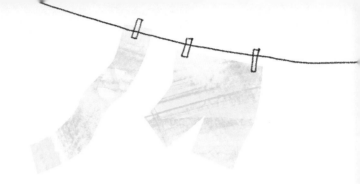

Enjoying your book so much that you know you're going to read until it's finished, even if you have to stay up all night.

The fresh smell of washing that's been drying out in the sunshine.

When you're melting at your desk and someone brings you an ice lolly. An actual ice lolly!

Doing something later than you were supposed to but thankfully no one has noticed.

Small acts of
kindness and grace.

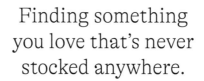

Finding something
you love that's never
stocked anywhere.

When a bunch of flowers
lasts for much longer than
you'd been expecting.

Returning from holiday
and the morbid relief that
you haven't been burgled.

The sound of rain hitting a tent.

The way ice pings and cracks when you pour a cold drink over it.

SUMMER

The smell of your skin after you've been in the sea.

SUMMER

Birdsong in the early evening.

AUTUMN

The precise time of year when the leaves are turning red and gold.

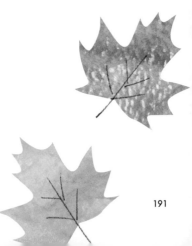

A nap on a rainy afternoon.

AUTUMN

Being in a place so remote that you can see every star in the sky.

The warmth of a mug of tea as you hold it in your hands.

Using twice the amount of garlic
than the recipe specifies.

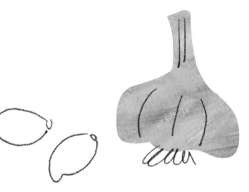

A beautiful word with no direct
English translation.

AUTUMN

Tsundoku, the process of incessantly filling your home with books.

Picking wild blackberries and eating the best ones as you go.

AUTUMN

Going for an early morning swim and you're the only person in the pool.

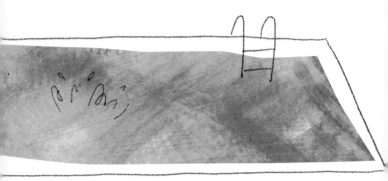

AUTUMN

A small window that can barely
manage all the sunlight trying
to burst through.

Placing the final piece
of a jigsaw puzzle.

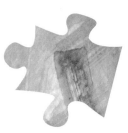

The first time someone
casually holds your hand,
just for a minute, as you
watch a movie together.

When you've been hungry all morning and it's finally lunchtime.

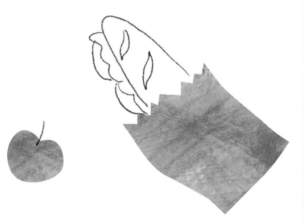

AUTUMN

Finding a book from your childhood that you'd completely forgotten about and it feels like running into an old friend.

Bioluminescence.

Petting a dog under the table.

The guilt lifting as you reply
to an email you've been putting
off for ages.

Sitting on the top deck of a bus
late at night, feeling peaceful.

When you try a complicated new recipe and it isn't a disaster.

Letting go of
something painful.

A book that's so great you can't
wait to tell people about it.

The squeak of trainers
on an indoor sports court.

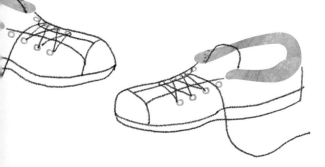

AUTUMN

A kiss on your collarbone.

Feeling certain that autumn
is the loveliest time of year.

AUTUMN

Having a shower in the morning
and then putting your pyjamas
back on afterwards.

Illuminating a room with
a few lamps instead of putting
the big light on.

AUTUMN

When you visit a bookshop
for the first time and want
to buy half of their stock.

When you've unknowingly dropped
something and a stranger runs
up to you holding it.

AUTUMN

Licking the spoon
when you're baking a cake.

A hot water bottle
on your lap.

Toast so buttery it's surely
some kind of crime.

AUTUMN

Easily finding the end
of a roll of sticky tape.

Sitting in a cafe with a good book and time on your hands.

When it's been raining all day
but it stops just long enough
to get home.

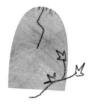

A walk around a Victorian cemetery that's being steadily reclaimed by nature.

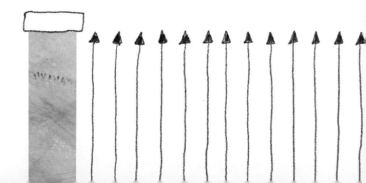

When you're indecisive about what to order at a restaurant and it turns out you made the right choice.

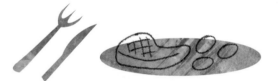

Getting out the house after you've been inside all day.

Finding two empty seats together
in a packed cinema.

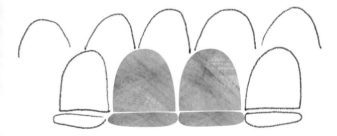

Coming home from a night out and making yourself an elaborate late-night snack.

A well-sharpened pencil.

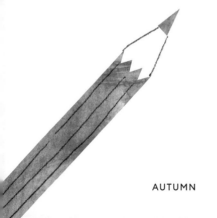

When it's cold enough to start wearing your favourite scarf again.

Getting into bed exhausted
and feeling yourself sink into
the mattress.

Spending an afternoon wandering
around an art gallery without
anywhere particular to be.

Free samples at the supermarket.

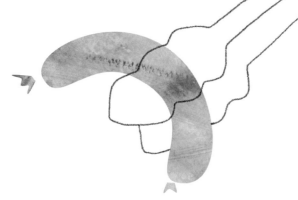

When a potential new friend
makes a reference to something
obscure you love.

Carrying several drinks back
from the bar and not spilling
any of them.

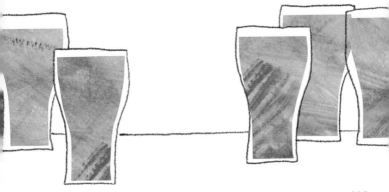

The names of rivers, always
so ancient and mysterious.

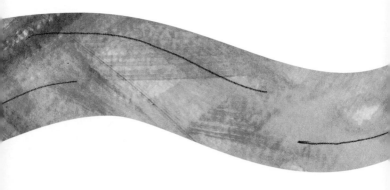

AUTUMN

Every last Muppet.

Scrunching up your toes
on a good carpet.

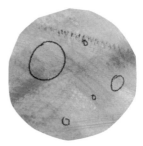

When it's morning but you
can still see the moon.

Returning to your kitchen moments before the timer goes off and feeling magnificently capable.

The cosy relief once you finally
decide to put the heating on.

When you think one of your plants has died but then it roars back to life.

An open bar.

Calling someone just
because it's comforting
to hear their voice.

When everyone has gone to bed and it feels like you're the only awake person in the world.

The smell of a bakery first thing
in the morning.

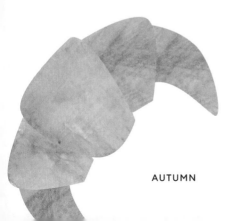

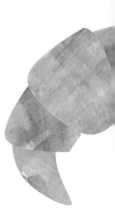

Meeting up with a friend just
to chat and kick some leaves
around the local park.

AUTUMN

A rainbow in an oily puddle,
a lowly miracle.

Seeing someone waiting for you on the platform as your train pulls into the station.

The word "spooktacular".

A bike ride along a river,
trying not to be distracted
by the burnished foliage.

When you're at a pub quiz and
you know the answer to a really
difficult question.

Finishing a really long book
and it feels like you've climbed
a mountain.

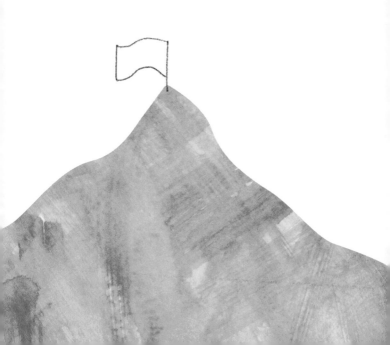

When a newly washed item of clothing is dry just in time for you to wear it out.

Walking through a wood as rain
taps on the canopy above.

Finally getting home on a
chilly day and leaning against
a radiator until you warm up.

AUTUMN

AUTUMN

Perfectly peeling the label
off a beer bottle.

When you suddenly remember you've been ill recently, which means that you're no longer ill.

Watching a cat out of the window, carefully plotting its way across the top of a fence.

Brevity.

The warmth of the bag of food as it sits in your lap on the ride home from the takeaway.

Being unexpectedly, deeply moved
by an object in a museum.

When someone compliments
you on an item of clothing
you've had for years.

Finally getting out of the car
on a long journey and stretching
your legs.

The quiet promise
of a brand new notebook.

When a friend bakes you something. I cannot stress enough how lovely this is.

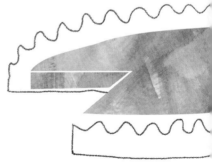

Completing a loyalty card that you've had since the dawn of time.

AUTUMN

When there's just enough tea left
in the pot for another cup.

Eating pizza without
burning the roof
of your mouth.

A perfect crescent moon
that looks like an old-fashioned
stage decoration.

Buying yourself flowers.

When you finally deep clean your fridge and you have a bounty of shelf space.

Arriving somewhere late and panicking, only to find that your friend is even later than you so it's okay.

Dressing up fancily even though
it's not a special occasion.

The fierce tingle in your chest
after a sip of whisky.

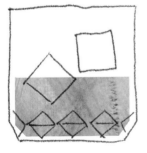

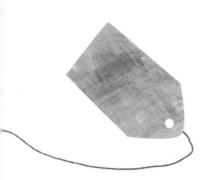

When the thing you were going to buy anyway turns out to be on sale.

Falling asleep in a car and waking up just as you arrive at your destination.

A shadow in your home
that only appears at
a certain time of day.

Dogs with jobs.

The simple pleasure of standing
in the dark and watching
fireworks, bundled up
in your warmest coat.

AUTUMN   279

WINTER

A freezing cold swim in the
sea that makes you thrum like
a just-rung bell.

Going to a pub and finding some empty chairs next to a roaring fire.

A cookbook that automatically
opens to your favourite recipe
because you've made it so often.

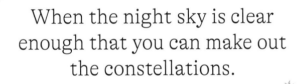

When the night sky is clear
enough that you can make out
the constellations.

Putting a hot water bottle under the sheets early so that your bed is toasty by the time you get in.

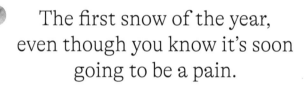

The first snow of the year,
even though you know it's soon
going to be a pain.

Spending a decent chunk of the morning thinking it's Thursday before realising that it's actually Friday.

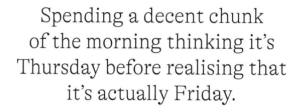

When you don't have to get up at a specific time so you let your body wake you naturally.

Breakfast food.

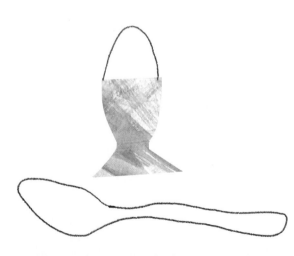

A bath that seems to last most
of the afternoon.

Finding a handwritten note as you open a second-hand book.

WINTER

Really thick, warm socks.

Frosted leaves of grass,
glinting in the sun.

❄ ❄ ❄

When you have a meal cooking
in the oven for hours and your
entire home smells heavenly.

Wearing fresh
pyjamas to bed.

Carrying a Christmas tree home,
feeling quietly festive.

When giant inflatable animals
break free of their tethers and
tumble down motorways.

Fog so thick it's like the world
has vanished.

Waking up slightly before your alarm goes off, so it feels like you have extra time in bed.

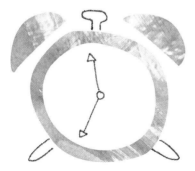

A friend calling just because they were thinking about you.

When you're the only person
in the cinema so it's like they're
screening the film just for you.

Looking out to sea and spotting
a tiny ship on the horizon.

When you're slicing some cheese for a meal and you leave yourself a little extra just to snack on.

The crunch of fresh snow
as you walk on it.

Returning home to a pet that's overjoyed to see you.

A compliment from
someone you admire.

When your phone has
just enough charge to
get through the day.

A new book and all
weekend to read it.

WINTER

Moving through your home in the middle of the night and the only illumination is the orange splash of a street light.

When, at long last, you've finished doing the dishes.

Eating cake mix straight out
of the bowl.

WINTER

The sound of scissors snipping decisively through thick paper.

WINTER

A good cry.

Wiping condensation from
a window with your sleeve
and looking out onto the street
below, like Scrooge after the
ghosts have visited.

When you're running for a bus
and the driver waits for you.

A freshly baked loaf of bread
that's still warm.

Having an excuse to use
an impressive word.

❄ ❄ ❄

Your family all under
the same roof for the first
time in ages.

The momentary flush of excitement when you slip a letter into a postbox.

Getting a strike in bowling despite the fact that you're usually a shambles.

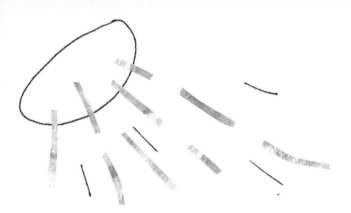

A shower that has the water
pressure of a hosepipe.

When someone is really pedantic about something you've said and it turns out you're actually right. Checkmate.

When frost makes the
pavement glitter.

Taking your duvet to the sofa
to spend a lazy day watching TV
and doing very little else.

A cat asleep on your lap,
its little belly rising and
falling contentedly.

When you find a strange and wonderful shop in a side street and it's almost as if you imagined it into being.

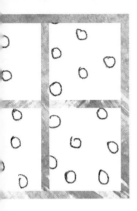

A warm cafe when
it's cold outside.

Peeling dried glue off
your fingertips.

When something makes you
laugh so much you're basically
useless for fifteen minutes.

Feeling excited about getting
a new cushion, even though
it's just a cushion.

Going for a drink with
your co-workers at the
end of a long day.

Crisp winter sunlight, pouring across the morning.

Watching a bad movie with
good friends.

A waterfall so imposing and august that you wish you were an 18th-century bard so you could write a stirring poem about it.

Using too much bubble bath and the tub is more bubble than bath.

WINTER

When you become briefly obsessed
with a song and have to listen
to it over and over again.

Getting through a difficult experience and feeling tougher and wiser for it.

An extra slice of toast.

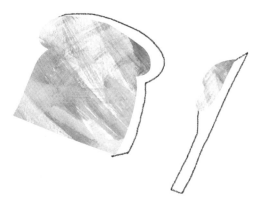

A haircut that makes you feel like
an entirely new version of yourself.

Putting on thick boots and
tramping through the woods.

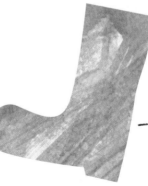

When the pattern on the
wrapping paper lines up perfectly
as you wrap a present.

WINTER

Unexpectedly getting
an afternoon off work.

Waking up to
snow-capped rooftops.

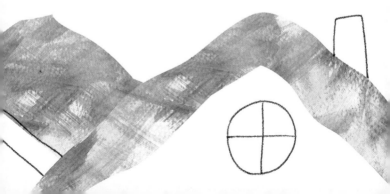

A jumper that
feels like a hug.

When you meet someone and have a sense that they're going to be a meaningful part of your life from this point on.

The smell of fresh herbs as you rub them between your fingers.

WINTER

Supporting your local library.

When the rain clears up all at once, and the sun comes out.

A proper sit down after spending
the day on your feet.

Stepping in an icy puddle
and hearing it crack.

WINTER

Being taken care of when you're feeling under the weather.

A dog that always seems
to be in a good mood.

Clasping your hands around
a mug of mulled wine.

Thinking something is going
to be impossible to fix but then
it turns out to be easy.

The way that a train ticket makes
a perfect bookmark.

When a friend is coming around so you bake some cookies, but it's really just because you fancy a cookie.

On a freezing day, seeing your breath plume out in front of you and feeling that life can be pretty romantic.

Working out the solution
to an annoying problem while
you're in the shower.

When the only light in the room is the Christmas tree.

Lying with your head on your partner's chest, their heart beating through their skin.

A sandwich that fulfils your very particular sandwich needs.

When a toddler curls up against
you as you read them a story.

WINTER

A long wintry walk, just for the pleasure of being outside.

Wearing a cardigan to bed.

WINTER

Collective nouns.

Wood crackling and popping
on a fire.

The pretty-much-magical way
that a cup of tea can always make
you feel just a little bit better.

A bridge that delights you every time you see it.

Feeling a little bit hopeful about the year ahead, and maybe that's enough.

Snow falling gently
on an empty street.

A quiet moment of optimism;
the chance to start again.

ACKNOWLEDGEMENTS

Thank you to Lara Watson for first encouraging me to write about small joys, and to Liz Bennett, Rosanna Durham and Alice Snape for their expertise, guidance and kindness over the years – I really should have included "A fine editor" somewhere in this book. Thanks also to Liz Seabrook and Hannah Hood (much missed) for their early enthusiasm, Emi Chiba, Susan Le and Katherine Zhang for their fabulous illustrations, and Kate Pollard for steering this project with her customary tenacity and skill. Finally, thanks to my parents and my siblings Amanda and Jonathan, who have always taught me the value of a chair with a great swivel action so you feel like a criminal mastermind whenever you spin around.

Published in 2022 by OH Editions
Part of Welbeck Publishing Group.
Based in London and Sydney.
www.welbeckpublishing.com

Design © 2022 OH Editions

Text © 2022 Jason Ward
Illustrations © 2022 Evi O Studio

UK ISBN 978-1-91431-766-8
US ISBN 978-1-80453-042-9

Publisher: Kate Pollard
Editor: Matt Tomlinson
Designer: Evi O Studio | Emi Chiba
Illustrators: Evi O Studio | Emi Chiba,
Susan Le & Katherine Zhang
Production controller: Arlene Alexander

Printed and bound
by RR Donnelley in China

MIX
Paper from
responsible sources
FSC® C020056

10 9 8 7 6 5 4 3 2 1